Celebrating your year

1954

a very special year for

_____

_____

_____

_____

_____

A message from the author:

Welcome to the year 1954.

I trust you will enjoy this fascinating romp down memory lane.

And when you have reached the end of the book, please join me in the battle against AI generated copy-cat books and fake reviews.

Details are at the back of the book.*

Best regards,
Bernard Bradforsand-Tyler.

* See page 81.

BULLY SENATE McCARTHY SILENCED

ERA of the SUPERIOR SUPERBOMBS

Rock 'n' Roll Shocks Parents!

Flashback to **1954** a very special year

Queen Elizabeth II 6-month Royal Tour

SALK'S VACCINE FIGHTS POLIO

BROWN BEATS BOARD OF EDUCATION

Walt Disney to build "The Happiest Place on Earth"

Contents

New *Airlight* Outdoor Telephone Booth—Larger, well-lighted and comfortable. Designed for use in all kinds of weather. Roof and frame are aluminum.

There's Something New in Telephone Booths

Any time you see one of these new *Airlight* Outdoor Telephone Booths you're likely to want to go right in and make a call.

For they are mighty attractive and comfortable. They are well-lighted, day and night. Tip-up directories are in easy reach. There's an ample shelf for packages and handbags.

The *Airlight* Outdoor Booths are never closed. They are available for service 24 hours a day, every day in the year.

It's just another step in the never-ending job of making the telephone more convenient and more useful to more and more people.

By bringing the telephone closer to you, we bring you closer to everybody. And thus make the service just that much more valuable.

Bell Telephone System

Reminding you that someone, somewhere, would enjoy hearing your voice today.

Let's flashback to 1954, a very special year.

Was this the year you were born?

Was this the year you were married?

Whatever the reason, this book is a celebration of your year,

THE YEAR 1954.

Turn the pages to discover a book packed with fun-filled
fabulous facts. We look at the people, the places, the
politics and the pleasures that made 1954 unique
and helped shape the world we know today.

So get your time-travel suit on, and enjoy this trip down memory
lane, to rediscover what life was like, back in the year 1954.

Imagine if time-travel was a reality, and one fine morning you wake up to find yourself flashed back in time, back to the year 1954.

What would life be like for a typical family, in a typical town, somewhere in America?

The post-war boom continued throughout the entire decade of the '50s. And with the booming economy, came booming birth numbers, booming suburbs, and the booming trappings of the consumerist culture we still live in today.

Our rising middle classes were feeling cashed-up. With an increasing desire to spend and to own, consumer demand continued to reach new highs year after year.

An unprecedented 4.07 million babies were born in 1954, the first time on record that annual births exceeded 4 million.[1]

To cater to the increase in population, new houses were built in record numbers, most of them in the new suburban developments springing up on the outskirts of towns. Home sales were boosted by returned soldiers who had access to low interest loans through the G.I. Bill (1944-1956). A house in the suburbs had become the American dream for white middle-class families.

Fathers commuted to earn a salary, while mothers were encouraged to quit their jobs and stay at home. Children walked to school and played outdoors in their well manicured gardens.

Joining the TV in our families' list of must-haves were: vacuum cleaners, washing machines, fully-automatic front-loading dryers, air-conditioning and heating units, defrost refrigerators, milkshake makers, and a multitude of other fancy kitchen gadgets and home appliances. In addition, every respectable family needed a car or two, motorcycles, bicycles, hiking/ camping/ picnic gear, and much, much more. An energetic and persuasive advertising industry, through TV, radio and print, ensured we always knew what our next purchase should be.

General Electric Spacemaker ad.

[1] U.S. Census Bureau *Provisional Estimates of the Population of the US: Jan 1, 1950, to March 1, 1955*.

More than 120 lbs. of frozen food easily stored in the big freezer section *at the bottom* of this new kind of refrigerator.

"Up-Side-Down" refrigerator!

Now—makers of famous Dual-Temp give you full family-size home
freezer and refrigerator—*all in one.* Never needs defrosting!

UP TOP—more storage capacity than in regular 9 cu. ft. refrigerator. Compare actual food-storage space of this new kind of refrigerator with any regular refrigerator. It's big! And it's all in easy-reach position—no bending or stooping.

AT THE BOTTOM—giant freezer holds 2¾ bushels of frozen food. Freezes food at 20° below zero—coldest cold of any refrigerator-freezer. Just right for *safe* quick freezing. Zero can be dialed for regular frozen food storage.

TWO TEMPERATURE CONTROLS—one for the Sub-Zero Freezer, one for the Humid Cold Compartment • **TWO ROLL OUT SHELVES**—easily cleaned, rust resistant • **ULTRA-VIOLET LAMP** in the humid-cold compartment helps purify the air, retards growth of mold and bacteria. See it at your Admiral Dealer's now.

Admiral Refrigerators start as low as $179.95

Makers of the famous Dual-Temp

"Up-Side-Down" refrigerator!

Now—makers of famous Dual-Temp give you full family-size home freezer and refrigerator—all in one. Never needs defrosting!

Up Top—more storage capacity than in regular 9 cu. ft. refrigerator. Compare actual food-storage space of this new kind of refrigerator with any regular refrigerator. It's big! And it's all in easy-reach position—no bending or stooping.

At the bottom—giant freezer holds $2^3/_4$ bushels of frozen food. Freezes food at 20° below zero—coldest cold of any refrigerator-freezer. Just right for *safe* quick freezing. Zero can be dialed for regular frozen food storage.

Two temperature controls—one for the Sub-Zero Freezer, one for the Humid Cold Compartment • Two roll out shelves—easily cleaned, rust resistant • Ultra-Violet Lamp in the humid-cold compartment helps purify the air, retards growth of mold and bacteria. See it at your Admiral Dealer's now.

Admiral Refrigerators start as low as $179.95.

Average costs in 1954 [1]	
New house	$18,281
Television	$150
Refrigerator	$330
Gasoline	$0.29 / gallon

The US economy suffered a short contraction during 1954, caused by the end of the Korean War and a reduction in war related spending and earnings. Unemployment rose to 5%. The average family income was $4,200 a year.[2]

Beneath the appearance of domestic bliss, Americans were deeply concerned. Civil rights activism was entering a new phase. From 1954 to 1968, the struggle for social justice intensified. Coordinated acts of non-violent civil disobedience gave African Americans a voice and national visibility.

Protesters in St. Louis, 1954.

A safety education magazine from the '50s.

McCarthyism peaked in 1954, as accusations of communist infiltrators touched all levels of government and society. By the end of the year, the tide of public opinion would turn against Senator McCarthy and his endless conspiracy theories.

The nuclear arms race between the USA and the Soviet Union intensified as Cold War fears gripped the nation. We would endure nearly four more decades of tension between the two super-powers before the Cold War ended in 1991 with the dissolution of the Soviet Union.

[1] thepeoplehistory.com and mclib.info/reference/local-history-genealogy/historic-prices/.
[2] census.gov/library/publications/1954/demo/p60-015.html.

Only Parker gives you both!

For the <u>seconds</u> you spend filling a pen   For the <u>years</u> you spend writing

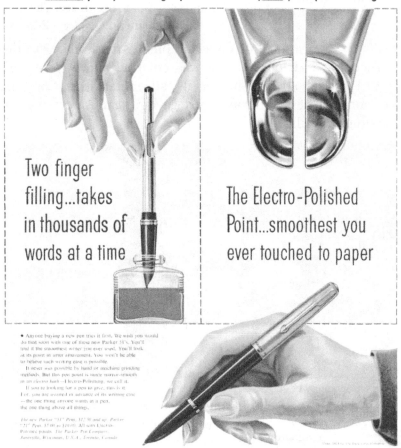

Two finger filling...takes in thousands of words at a time

The Electro-Polished Point...smoothest you ever touched to paper

Only Parker gives you both!

For the seconds you spend filling a pen...For the years you spend writing.

Two finger filling...takes in thousands of words at a time.

The Electro-Polished Point...smoothest you ever touched to paper.

Anyone buying a new pen tries it first. We wish you would do that soon with one of these new Parker 51's. You'll find it the smoothest writer you ever used. You'll look at its point in utter amazement. You won't be able to believe such writing ease is possible.

It never was possible by hand or machine grinding methods. But this pen point is made mirror-smooth in an *electro bath*–Electro-Polishing, we call it.

If you're looking for a pen to give, this is it. For, you are assured in advance of its writing ease–the one thing anyone wants in a pen, the one thing above all things.

The new Parker "51" Pens, $12.50 and up. Parker "21" Pens, $5.00 to $10.00.

All with Electro-Polished points. The Parker Pen Company, Jamesville, Wisconsin, USA; Toronto, Canada.

Now just imagine you flashed back to a town
in 1954 United Kingdom or Western Europe.

Unlike boom-time America, a very different
picture would await you.

Many major cities like London bore the brunt of destruction from
WWII bombings. The post-war rebuilding process required major
loans from the USA and other nations, leaving the UK deep in long-
term debt. Reconstruction was painfully slow, hampered by a general
shortage of money, manpower and materials. The substantial loans
took decades to repay, and were finally paid back in full in 2006.

A central London street in the mid-'50s.

In most British cities there was a desperate
shortage of housing to accommodate the
growing population. Nearly half of those living
in cities rented private, often substandard
apartments. While in the country, homes often
lacked water, sanitation, electricity and phones.

The post-war baby boom, along with the shortage of funds and building materials for new schools, often resulted in crowded classes of up to 50 students in urban areas.

British children at school in the early '50s.

Stifling and miserable austerity measures had been in place since the start of the war, affecting everything from fabrics to food. During the early '50s restrictions had slowly been lifted, with the last controlled item—the rationing of meat—lifted on 4th July 1954.

Finally free from austerity restrictions, the British populace was feeling the positive winds of change. Job security and record low unemployment saw the middle and working classes feeling more prosperous and optimistic. Living standards were rising and families had money to spend.

'50s Aerial view of London showing bombed areas in the foreground.

Students! Parents!
"96-YEAR TEST" PROVES RUGGED ROYAL PERFECT GRADUATION PRESENT

For school, for college, for life—you want a *rugged* portable.

That is why Royal took a stock model and ran it for 2000 grueling hours at United States Testing Company in Hoboken, New Jersey.*

This punishment means this: you would have to write a 400-word letter or theme every day in the year (except Sundays) for 96 years to equal the workout this stock model Royal received. With Royal Portable you get a typewriter, useful for the rest of your life.

Proved ruggedness like this costs only $9.95 down with 18 months to pay. Liberal trade-ins. To own this top notch portable typewriter see your Royal Portable dealer today.

> **These 10 amazing features make Royal do more for you . . . do it better!**
>
> Speed Selector • New Speed Spacer • Push Button Top • Visible Tab Set • New Color Combinations • New Carriage Controls • Greater Paper Capacity • Fiberglas-plastic Carrying Case • Line Meter • plus Royal's famous "Magic" Margin.

*Test Number E-4998, Oct. 14, 1953.

Give the new rugged **ROYAL** portable
. . . the typewriter of a lifetime for a lifetime

Students! Parents!
"96-year test" proves rugged Royal perfect graduation present

For school, for college, for life–you want a *rugged* portable.

That is why Royal took a stock model and ran it for 2000 grueling hours at United States Testing Company in Hoboken, New Jersey.

This punishment means this: you would have to write a 400-word letter or theme every day in the year (except Sundays) for 96 years to equal the workout this stock model Royal received. With Royal Portable you get a typewriter, useful for the rest of your life.

Proved ruggedness like this costs only $9.95 down with 18 months to pay. Liberal trade-ins. To own this top-notch portable typewriter see your Royal Portable dealer today.

Give the new rugged Royal portable
...the typewriter of a lifetime for a lifetime

Queen Elizabeth II was just 25 years old when she ascended to the throne in June 1953. Five months after her coronation, the Queen and her husband embarked on a six-month Royal Tour of 13 far-flung Commonwealth realms—from the Caribbean, to Oceania, Asia and Africa. This included longer stays in Australia (8 weeks) and New Zealand (6 weeks), two countries which had never before hosted a member of the Royal family. The Royal Tour ended in May 1954.

Winston Churchill, UK Prime Minister from 1940-1945, returned for a second term in 1951 at almost 77 years old.

In November 1954, to celebrate his 80th birthday, members of Parliament commissioned artist Graham Sutherland to paint a full length portrait of Churchill. Churchill disliked the unflattering painting so much he had it transferred to his country house, then arranged for it to be destroyed.

1954 portrait of Winston Churchill by Graham Sutherland.

Churchill with Queen Elizabeth II, Prince Charles and Princess Anne, 10th Feb 1953.

Churchill's health had been declining for many years. In June 1953, he suffered a stroke causing partial paralysis. Although Churchill continued working until his retirement in 1955, he kept his stroke hidden from the public.

Lack of excess cash reserves made it increasingly difficult for the UK to continue financing and keeping secure its far-flung colonies. As a result, many British colonies would be released during the following 10 years, gaining independence as new nations. The United Kingdom was quickly losing its super-power status on the world's stage.

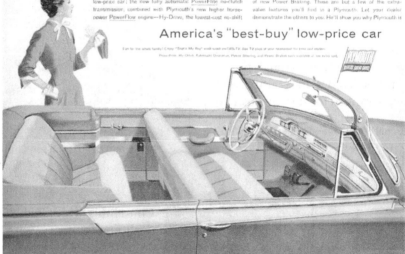
Take a close look at the Beauty and a long view of the Value!
New '54 Plymouth

The fresh, high-spirited look of a new 1954 Plymouth draws admiring eyes everywhere it goes. And behind its wheel you begin to appreciate the value that lies beneath its beauty.

There's the widest choice of drives ever offered by any low-price car: the new fully automatic PowerFlite no-clutch transmission, combined with Plymouth's new higher horse-power PowerFlow engine–Hy-Drive, the lowest-cost no-shift driving–Automatic Overdrive–and, of course, Plymouth's famous Synchro-Silent transmission.

Also, there's the energy-saving ease and convenience of full-time Power Steering. The added sureness and security of new Power Braking. These are but a few of the extra-value features you'll find in a Plymouth. Let your dealer demonstrate the others to you. He'll show you why Plymouth is America's "best-buy" low-price car.

Our Love Affair with Cars

By 1954, the US dominated the world's car market, fabricating more than half of all new vehicles internationally. In less than ten years, the car industry had shifted from supplying utilitarian war tanks and trucks, to producing fashionable consumer vehicles, the kind of which we just had to have.

An additional two million vehicles were put on US roads during 1954 as families fled the cities for the quiet life of the suburbs. There were now 48.3 million registered cars on US roads, up from 25.7 million at the end of WWII.[1]

Mid-Afternoon Traffic on Broad Street, Philadelphia, early '50s.

Teenagers at a drive-through in the mid-'50s.

Services related business such as drive-through restaurants and drive-in cinemas were springing up everywhere, especially popular among the younger generation.

[1] fhwa.dot.gov/ohim/summary95/mv200.pdf.
[2] en.wikipedia.org/wiki/American_automobile_industry_in_the_1950s.
[3] theweek.com/articles/461968/rise-fall-detroit-timeline.

1954 Mercury Monterey Convertible.

1954 Dodge Royal V-8 Four-Door Sedan.

Our love affair with cars grew hand-in-hand with the post-war baby boom and housing construction boom. Where would we be without our cars? How else could we commute from our outer-suburban homes to our inner-city offices?

Rising incomes ensured the family car was increasingly affordable. The rising middle class had money to spend, and cars became the ultimate status symbol.

Cars were no longer just a necessity; they had become an expression of our personality. Car manufacturers competed for our attention with stylish designs, larger engines, and added detailing. Luxurious, sturdy, or sporty, cars now came in a wide range of styles, colors, and price points, with chrome, wings, stripes and fins for added pizzaz.

1954 Buick Special.

Four car-producing countries dominated the industry by the start of 1954: England, France, and Germany, with America in the top spot. (Japan had yet to enter this elite group.)

Right: Renault 4CV, 1954.
Below: MG Magnette, 1954.

SPORTS-CAR **PERFORMANCE!**
FAMILY-CAR **COMFORT!**
SMALL-CAR **ECONOMY!**

4 DOOR SEDAN

MG *MAGNETTE*

American car manufacturers produced 8 million vehicles in 1954 alone, accounting for more than 90% of cars sold in the country.

Detroit was America's car production powerhouse, where car manufacturers produced year-on-year bigger, longer and heavier gas-guzzlers to satisfy the '50s consumer desire for power and style over efficiency and safety. "The Big Three" (General Motors, Chrysler and Ford) dominated the industry, having bought out or edged out most of their competitors.

Detroit had become the fifth largest city in the US, and by the end of the decade, a whopping one in six American adults would be employed in the car industry nation-wide.[1]

GM Chevrolet assembly line in the mid '50s.

[1] theweek.com/articles/461968/
rise-fall-detroit-timeline.

The one car that befits the occasion!

There are nineteen different makes of motor cars manufactured in the land today. And yet, the overwhelming majority of motorists would agree that only one is perfectly appropriate for the distinguished occasion pictured above.

That car—as you surely know—is Cadillac!

And you could safely predict that at any such occasion...or in any of the season's proudest social events...or at any of the year's most significant affairs of state...the Cadillacs would be in dominant attendance!

But it is important to remember that a Cadillac also belongs in far less pretentious surroundings. For with its great beauty, its superlative performance and its magnificent luxury—the Cadillac car also offers unusual dependability, remarkable operating economy and extraordinary value.

That, we think you will agree, is a combination worth your personal consideration. Won't you stop in soon and let us give you the full, wonderful Cadillac story?

It is entirely possible that a Cadillac belongs in *your* driveway!

Your Cadillac Dealer

Styled by world famous Raymond Loewy!

World's most beautiful station wagon!

Get a far-advanced '54 Studebaker
and enjoy the pride of driving
the most modern car in America

Studebaker is first in America in sports car design!

Get ahead of the parade...get more when you trade.

Be sure that you don't settle for an old-fashioned "new" car this year. Get the out-ahead smartness of the most modern automobile in America—the exciting '54 Studebaker.

Studebaker's speedlined new low silhouette is more than the greatest advance ever made in car styling. It's like money in the bank as insurance of top trade-in value.

Better still, the pace-setting new Studebaker design helps to cut your driving costs 'way down. You stop paying the price of gas-eating excess bulk and power-wasting dead weight.

'54 Mobilgas Economy Run winner!

Three 1954 Studebakers rolled up sensational victories in this year's Mobilgas Run. Studebaker won the Grand Sweepstakes Award—finished first in actual miles per gallon and ton miles per gallon. Try out the '54 Champion or Commander V-8 at your nearby Studebaker dealer's.

Styled by world famous Raymond Loewy. World's most beautiful station wagon!

Get a far-advanced '54 Studebaker and enjoy the pride of driving the most modern car in America.

Studebaker is first in America in sports car design!

The Golden Age of Television

During the 1950s, the television quickly became the centerpiece of every family home. By 1954, at least half the homes in the USA owned a television set, (up from just 9% in 1950). And in the UK, TV sets were found in at least a quarter of all homes. TV ownership continued to rise exponentially as television became our preferred choice of entertainment.

For the rising middle classes, television was much more convenient than going to a downtown cinema. It provided an increasing array of programs to watch, was available every day of the week, and it was free to watch once purchased. The rise of television spelled doom for the motion-picture industry. Cinema going audiences deserted downtown movie theaters in droves, forcing many to close.

Most Popular Television Shows of 1954

1	I Love Lucy	11	The Buick-Berle Show
2	The Jackie Gleason Show	12	This Is Your Life
3	Dragnet	13	I've Got a Secret
4	You Bet Your Life	14	Two for the Money
5	The Toast of the Town	15	Your Hit Parade
6	Disneyland	16	The Millionaire
7	The Jack Benny Show	17	General Electric Theater
8	The George Gobel Show	18	Arthur Godfrey's Talent Scouts
9	Ford Theatre	19	Private Secretary
10	December Bride	20	Fireside Theatre

* From the Nielsen Media Research 1954-'55 season of top-rated USA primetime television series.

During the first half of the 1950s, live television broadcasts from New York City dominated, based on radio and the theatrical traditions of Broadway. These were faster and cheaper to produce than new made-for-TV programs. However, situation-comedies, soap operas, and dramas, mostly created in Los Angeles, would soon become our primetime staples.

Lucille Ball with real life husband Desi Arnaz in *I Love Lucy* (CBS. 1950-1955).

Jack Webb (Sergeant Joe Friday) and Harry Morgan in *Dragnet* (NBC. 1951-1959).

Variety shows, game shows, and situation-comedies remained the most popular forms of family-time TV entertainment, accounting for 13 of the top 20 programs of 1954.

Also keeping us glued to our TVs were highly rated drama series such as *Ford Theatre* (NBC, ABC. 1948-'57), *Dragnet* (NBC. 1951-'59), and *Fireside* (NBC. 1949-'58).

Steve Allen as host of *Tonight* (later *The Tonight Show,* NBC. 1954-present).

Jan Clayton, George Cleveland, and Tommy Rettig with Lassie in *Lassie* (CBS. 1954).

The television networks were quick to turn out new programs to keep us tuning in. Here are just a few of the new programs that aired for the first time in 1954: *Disneyland* (later *The Wonderful World of Disney*), *Father Knows Best, Howdy Doody, It's Wallace?, NBA on NBC, Lassie, Zoo Quest* (BBC.), *The Tonight Show* (NBC. 1954-present), and *Face the Nation* (CBS. 1954-present).

David Attenborough's first TV series, as host of nature program *Zoo Quest* (BBC. 1954-'63).

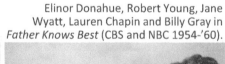

Elinor Donahue, Robert Young, Jane Wyatt, Lauren Chapin and Billy Gray in *Father Knows Best* (CBS and NBC 1954-'60).

Shop Look Listen-and you'll buy Emerson TV

Choose from 60 distinctive 17", 21" and 27" models priced from $129.95

Shop for value!

Best monochrome reception of all programs, including color!

Superb quality at prices so low you can afford a set for every room!

Powerful, built-in, pre-tuned antenna—no outdoor antenna needed in most areas!

Look at the picture! Look at the style!

New Cinevision picture...so clear, so sharp...you'll think you're at the movies!

Powerful performance wherever you live!

Only Emerson's five "Decoright" finishes match your furniture exactly!

Listen to the high fidelity performance!

Emerson's Full Fidelity sound system recreates the artist in your home!

One Knob Simplimatic tuning locks in sound and picture automatically!

Emerson.

Over 15,000,000 satisfied owners prove Emerson is America's Best Buy!

Castle Bravo and the Superior Superbombs

Cold War tensions between the two former allies–the USSR and the USA–dominated our lives throughout the '50s and '60s. Starting in the USA as policies for communist containment, the distrust and misunderstanding between the two sides quickly escalated from political squabbling, to a military nuclear arms race. For more than 40 years, the Nuclear Arms Race gave the two superpowers the pretext needed to test nuclear bombs on a massive scale.

At the end of 1952, the USA flexed its nuclear muscle by detonating the world's first superbomb–a H-bomb (thermonuclear fusion hydrogen bomb)– one hundred times more powerful than the atomic bombs dropped on Hiroshima and Nagasaki. Code-named *Ivy Mike*, at 82 tons, it was too heavy to be deployed by air.

Ivy Mike, detonated at Enewetak Atoll in the Marshall Islands, Pacific Ocean, 1st Nov 1952.

By 1954, the US had developed lighter, aircraft-deliverable H-bombs. Testing took place through a series of detonations in and around the Marshall Islands' Bikini Atoll, located in the Pacific Ocean. During March and April '54, a series of seven tests took place, each using different "wet" or "dry" fuels in varied concentrations. Devices ranged in weight from 6,520 to 39,600 pounds (2,960 to 17,960 kg).

The first test, codenamed Castle Bravo, detonated on 1st March 1954. The resulting 15 megaton blast was 2.5 times larger than the bomb designers had predicted, due to flawed assumptions and calculation errors. The yield was one thousand times more powerful than the Hiroshima and Nagasaki bombs.

Castle Bravo mushroom cloud with vapor rings, Bikini Atoll, Marshall Islands, Pacific Ocean, 1st Mar 1954.

A mushroom cloud 4.5 miles (7.2 km) wide formed, reaching 130,000 feet (39.6 km) high. The blast left a 6,500 ft (2 km) wide, 250 ft (76 m) deep crater in the ocean floor.

The ensuing fallout spread radioactive debris 7,000 square miles (18,130 sq km) across the Pacific, contaminating the habitants of surrounding islands, crew of a Japanese fishing vessel, and US servicemen and scientists taking part in the tests. The affected people would be haunted by health problems for decades afterwards, including birth defects and cancers.

Days after the blast, Marshal Islanders were evacuated to other islands and are still unable to return home. Tragic stories circulated of children playing in the powdery radioactive fallout, unaware of the danger. Traces of radioactive material were discovered in Australia, India, Japan, and as far as the USA and Europe, precipitating calls for a ban on atmospheric testing.

Castle Bravo remains the largest ever US nuclear explosion. Three weeks later, Castle Yankee yielded 13.5 megatons, making it the second largest. The Soviets responded with four even more powerful H-bombs, including Tsar Bomba (1961) at 50 megatons.

With both sides H-bomb capable, Americans feared a nuclear war could start at any time. Citizens built bomb shelters, and nuclear bomb drills became commonplace.

Both superpowers continued to increase their nuclear weapon stockpiles. The US stockpile peaked in 1966 with a total of 31,175 against the Soviet's 7,089 weapons.[1] The USSR continued to grow their stockpile until 1988. In 1991, the Nuclear Arms Race ended with the signing of the denuclearization treaty.

School children crawl under their desks in a "duck and take cover" drill.

[1] tandfonline.com/doi/pdf/ 10.2968/066004008.

McCarthyism and the Red Scare

The "Red Scare" gripped Americans in the decade following the end of WWII. It described the paranoia, bordering on hysteria, caused by extreme fear of communist infiltration, influence, and attacks on US soil. Also known as McCarthyism, anyone accused of being liberal, leftist, socialist, communist or anti-American, could be investigated by the House Un-American Activities Committee (HUAC).

The HUAC crusade was spearheaded by Joseph McCarthy—a first term senator with a knack for firing-off sensational, highly publicized accusations.

Eisenhower Urges Anti-Red Crusade
Expose Poisonous Propaganda, President's Plea to Publishers

26 Teachers Are Suspended Here For Refusing to Answer Red Quiz

M'CARTHY NAMES ANOTHER U.S. OFFICIAL

M'Carthy Charges Reds Hold U.S. Jobs

HUAC INVESTIGATES "RED KLOWN": STARS TESTIFY

3,000 Arrested in Nation-Wide Round-Up of 'Reds': Palmer Directs Raids in 35 Cities; 650 Seized Here

Headlines from 1953-'54.

The HUAC specifically targeted government institutions and Hollywood's movie industry. Even hearsay or vague insinuations of disloyalty were enough to have one dragged before the HUAC for scrutiny. Few dared to criticize McCarthy's aggressive interrogation tactics, even where no proof of subversive activity existed. Although McCarthy failed to make a credible case against anyone, more than 2,000 government employees lost their jobs as a result of his public denunciations. Under pressure from the HUAC, movie studios created Hollywood blacklists that barred suspected radicals. Directors, broadcasters, writers, academics, and unionists also found themselves blacklisted. Most were never able to resume their careers even after the blacklists had been lifted.

From left: Leonard Bernstein, Orson Wells, and Lena Horne were some of the more than 300 writers, actors, singers and directors who were blacklisted.

At the start of 1954, McCarthy turned his attention to the US military. President Eisenhower fought back, invoking executive privilege to ban any White House or executive branch employees from testifying before the HUAC. With the first stone cast, McCarthy's fellow senators began to turn against him.

McCarthy testifying on Communist Party organization in the US, at the Army-McCarthy hearings, 9th June 1954.

When the US Army accused Senator McCarthy of improper conduct concerning favorable treatment of an aide, the resulting 36-day hearing was broadcast live nationally. Although unrelated to his anti-communist crusade, the hearings exposed McCarthy's aggressive and dishonest bullying tactics, turning public opinion against him.

In December 1954, the Senate passed a motion of condemnation against McCarthy for conduct "contrary to Senate traditions". Senator McCarthy died three years later, aged 47, from alcohol abuse.

The term McCarthyism has since entered the English vocabulary to describe baseless defamation or political witch-hunts without sufficient evidence, aimed to suppress opposition.

Newspaper headlines from 1954.

DAY, JUNE 10, 1954.   FIVE CENTS

WELCH ASSAILS M'CARTHY'S 'CRUELTY' AND 'RECKLESSNESS' IN ATTACK ON AIDE; SENATOR, ON STAND, TELLS OF RED HUNT

DECEMBER 3, 1954.   FIVE CENTS

FINAL VOTE CONDEMNS M'CARTHY, 67-22, FOR ABUSING SENATE AND COMMITTEE;

M'CARTHY ON STAND IN BITTER SCENE

AY, MARCH 12, 1954.   FIVE CENTS

ARMY CHARGES M'CARTHY AND COHN THREATENED IT IN TRYING TO OBTAIN PREFERRED TREATMENT FOR SCHINE

Tearful Welch Says Senator Reckless, 'Lacks Decency'

Vote Is Unanimous to Censure McCarthy

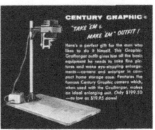

Brown vs Board of Education

On 17th May 1954, the US Supreme Court ruled in the case of Brown vs. Board of Education, that state based racial segregation in public schools was unconstitutional. This was a major victory for civil rights activists, instigating a new chapter in the Civil Rights Movement that would span from 1954 to 1968.

Lawyers George E.C. Hayes, Thurgood Marshall, and James M. Nabrit, Jr., celebrating outside the US Supreme Court, Washington, D.C., 17th May, 1954.

"Brown" was in fact five separate cases brought before the Supreme Court, all challenging the principle of "separate but equal" racial segregation in the public school system. The court's unanimous 9-0 decision found that segregated public education was inherently unequal.

States with laws promoting segregation, especially those in the deep South, refused to de-segregate. Although it would be decades before real strides were taken to achieve full school desegregation, Brown is still regarded as a landmark decision, setting a notable legal precedent with huge social impact.

A new direction in the Civil Rights Movement was launched, shifting from political lobbying to non-violent direct action. Sit-ins, boycotts, marches, protests, freedom rides, and acts of civil disobedience would become hallmarks of the Movement.

Press photo taken in 1964 to mark 10 years since Brown vs. Board. From left: Harry Briggs, Jr., Linda Brown Smith, and Spottswood Bolling, Jr., three students at the center of the five Supreme Court cases. On right is Briggs' mother Ethel Louise Belton Brown.

From 26th April to 21st July, the Geneva Conference united representatives from North Korea, South Korea, North Vietnam, South Vietnam, Cambodia, Laos, China, the Soviet Union, France, USA, and UK, with the aim of resolving outstanding disputes resulting from the Korean War and Indochina War.

The Geneva Conference, 1954.

Concerning Korea, the conference failed to provide any solution to reunite and bring peace to the Korean Peninsula. Numerous conflicting proposals were offered, debated, and rejected. To date, there has been no formal peace treaty, leaving the two Koreas technically still at war. The 1953 armistice along the 38th Parallel would unofficially become a de facto international border known as the demilitarized zone.

For Indochina, France officially withdrew from Vietnam following its shattering defeat by the communist backed North Vietnamese guerrilla army on 7th May 1954. The next day, negotiations began at the Geneva Conference to decide the future of the former French colonies in South East Asia.

Map of the partition of Indochina that resulted from the Geneva Conference.

By 21st July, the delegates had produced ten documents (the Accords). It was agreed that communist troops would withdraw from the ex-French colonies of Laos and Cambodia, and that a cease-fire would occur along the 17th parallel in Vietnam, temporarily dividing the country until elections for a united government could be held within two years.

Unfortunately, the Geneva Accords were not binding. Elections did not occur. Vietnam entered a 20-year-long civil war with the south aided by the USA and the north aided by China and the Soviets. The country was eventually reunited under communist rule following the Fall of Saigon in 1975.

Leave New York at noon–reach Los Angeles before 5p.m.
on United Air Lines' DC-7s, nonstop coast to coast!

Already in Service nonstop between San Francisco and New York, United's de luxe DC-7 Mainliners will also offer, starting July 1, nonstop flights between New York and Los Angeles. You leave New York on "the Continental" at noon, arrive in Los Angeles at 4:55 p.m. (local times). Eastbound it's only 7$^{1}/_{4}$ hours nonstop!

Also starting July 1: nonstop DC-7 service between Chicago and these cities: San Francisco, Los Angeles, New York. You can enjoy the finest coast-to-coast travel in history on United Air Lines' DC-7s–including the only nonstop flights from San Francisco to New York, fastest by over an hour, and the fastest service, also, from Manhattan to the Golden Gate.

Along with this new, magic speed–superb comfort! Full-course meals prepared by United's famous chefs...beverages and other enjoyable "extras"...a roomy, panoramic-view lounge...extra-fast luggage delivery from a special baggage compartment adjoining the main cabin (a United exclusive)...many other new ideas that make United's DC-7s the finest in the sky!

The Main Line Airway–to 80 Cities

Disneyland Commences Construction

Disneyland, Walt Disney's "folly" of fun, fantasy and futurism, began construction on 160 acres (65 ha) of land in Anaheim, southeast of Los Angeles, in July 1954.

Artist Herb Ryman helped to sketch Disney's ideas.

After several years of planning, the ambitious $17 million project was constructed in just one year. Despite an overcrowded and disastrous opening day, workers ensured all the park attractions were running smoothly within the month. And by the second month of operation, it was reported that 1 million people had visited. For most, it was and still is, "the happiest place on earth."

Above left: Walt Disney at the opening ceremony. "To all who come to this happy place–welcome. Disneyland is your land."

Above: Walt Disney (center) showing Orange County officials the plans for Disneyland's layout, December 1954.

Left: On 17th July 1955, an estimated 70 million people tuned in to watch ABC TVs 90-minute live broadcast of the star-studded opening ceremonies, co-hosted by Ronald Reagan.

A Vaccine for Polio

During the first half of the 20th Century, the dreaded poliomyelitis virus (polio) caused frequent epidemics throughout the industrialized world. The virus appeared during the summer months, attacking mostly the young, causing muscle weakness, paralysis and death. More than 75,000 polio cases were reported worldwide in 1954, with at least half in the USA alone.

On 6th April '74, the long awaited vaccine created by American medical researcher Dr. Jonas Salk, began large scale testing across the US, Canada, and Finland. By 1955, Dr. Salk's inactivated polio vaccine was licensed for use, providing 90% immunity against the virus after just two doses.

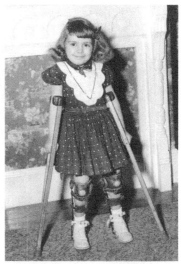

Polio patient–Elaine Burns, age 5, with her braces in 1957.

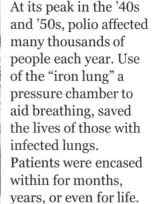

At its peak in the '40s and '50s, polio affected many thousands of people each year. Use of the "iron lung" a pressure chamber to aid breathing, saved the lives of those with infected lungs. Patients were encased within for months, years, or even for life.

Rows of polio patients in their iron lungs at the Rancho Los Amigos hospital in Downey, Calif. 1953.

To save on floor space within polio wards, children were placed in iron lung "pods"– multi-person negative-pressure ventilators.

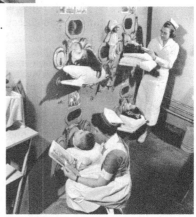

Worldwide polio eradication is still an ongoing struggle, as yearly outbreaks continue in some developing countries. Civil wars, ignorance, and government distrust prevent large scale vaccination programs from succeeding.

New National Accounting Machine Models

Now! money-saving accounting for more businesses—small and large

These newest National Accounting Machine models widen the field of businesses that can cut costs and speed their work.

National Accounting is now available with up to 17 totals. Some models, with fewer totals and features, are priced within easy range of the small or medium-size business.

All of these new models are available with or without Electric Typewriter.

Operators like National Accounting Machines because they learn to operate them so quickly...and are happier because they do their work more easily.

National Accounting Machines, in thousands of concerns, have paid for themselves in less than a year, and now continue savings as an annual profit. These new models bring such savings to many more businesses, small and large.

Investigate these new Nationals. See how the model and features suited to *your* needs can do your accounting at less cost, and give you valuable information *on time* as an extra bonus. Phone your nearest National representative—today!

National. Accounting Machines. Adding Machines. Cash Registers.

Miles Apart yet Heart-to-Heart by Long Distance

When you're far away from someone, there's nothing like a telephone call to bring you near. The sound of a warm, familiar voice and the eager exchange of personal news is almost as satisfying as an actual visit.

Near or far, wherever they are, friends appreciate your calling. Long Distance calls cost little–especially after six every evening and all day Sunday. Then you can talk from Cleveland to Detroit for as little as 40¢; Chicago to Omaha for only 85¢; New York to Los Angeles for only $2. (These are the 3-minute, station-to-station rates and do not include federal excise tax.)

Somewhere today there is someone who would like to hear your voice.

You save time when you call by number. When you're calling out-of-town, it will speed your call if you can give the operator the number you want.

Bell Telephone System

1954 in Cinema and Film

Having reached its peak in the mid-1940s, cinema attendance faced a steady decline throughout the 1950s. With more and more families filling their leisure time with the convenience of television, the motion-picture industry sought new ways to win over new audiences.

Younger audiences now had cash to spare. Movie themes adjusted to accommodate the trends in popular culture, and to exploit the sex appeal of young, rising stars such as Audrey Hepburn, Grace Kelly, James Dean, Marlon Brando, and Marilyn Monroe.

Elia Kazan's *On the Waterfront* starred teen idol Marlon Brando alongside Eva Marie Saint in her film debut role. Brando's raw and intense performance helped popularize "method acting"—using immersive emotional experience to prepare for the role. The film won eight Oscars from twelve nominations, including Best Picture, Best Actor, Best Actress and Best Director.

Highest Paid Stars

1	John Wayne
2	Dean Martin
=	Jerry Lewis
4	Gary Cooper
5	James Stewart
6	Marilyn Monroe
7	Alan Ladd
8	William Holden

1954 film debuts

Ursula Andress	An American in Rome
Sean Connery	Lilacs in the Spring
Jack Lemmon	It Should Happen to You
Eva Marie Saint	On the Waterfront
Roger Moore	The Last Time I Saw Paris
Paul Newman	The Silver Chalice
Kim Novak	The French Line
Omar Sharif	Devil of the Sahara

* From en.wikipedia.org/wiki/1954_in_film.

Top Grossing Films of the Year

1	White Christmas	Paramount Pictures	$12,000,000
2	The Caine Mutiny	Columbia Pictures	$8,700,000
3	20,000 Leagues Under the Sea	Disney/Buena Vista	$8,000,000
4	The Glenn Miller Story	Universal Pictures	$7,600,000
5	The Country Girl	Paramount Pictures	$6,500,000
6	The High and the Mighty	Warner Bros.	$6,100,000
=	A Star Is Born	Warner Bros.	$6,100,000
8	Seven Brides for Seven Brothers	MGM	$5,526,000
9	Rear Window	Paramount Pictures	$5,300,000
10	Magnificent Obsession	Universal Pictures	$5,200,000

* From en.wikipedia.org/wiki/1954_in_film by box office gross in the USA.

The mystery thriller *Rear Window* is considered to be the most gripping and suspenseful film by acclaimed director Alfred Hitchcock, and continues to rank among the greatest films ever made.

The feel-good holiday musical *White Christmas*, featuring the songs of Irving Berlin, was the first movie to be released on widescreen format VistaVision.

Best we can do here is "stop" the action. But with your Brownie Movie Camera, *you* can capture your youngsters in *moving* pictures . . . with *all* the action, *all* the color, *all* the reality of life itself.

Cost? A single roll of 8mm. color film makes 30 to 40 average-length scenes . . . costs only $3.95 *including processing!*
Ease? With the Brownie Movie Camera, home movies are simple as snapshots. But get the whole story for yourself from your Kodak dealer.

Movies at snapshot cost!

Brownie Movie Camera
only $39.75*

Loads easily—no threading. Built-in exposure guide . . . fine, fast *f*/2.7 lens. Unbeatably low priced at $39.75. Same camera with super-speed *f*/1.9 lens, only $49.50. Either model gives you sharp, clear, full-color movies at the touch of a button. See the "Brownies" soon.

*Many Kodak dealers offer convenient terms

"Brownie" movies start to finish! Brownie Movie Projector shows all 8mm. movies crisp, bright . . . stills, reverse action, too! Only $62.50. Brownie Projection Screen . . . beaded . . . a full 30 inches wide. $4.50.

Prices subject to change without notice and include Federal Tax where applicable

Action and only a movie camera can get it all!

Best we can do here is "stop" the action. But with your Brownie Movie Camera, *you* can capture your youngsters in *moving* pictures...with *all* the reality of life itself.

Cost? A single roll of 8mm. color film makes 30 to 40 average-length scenes...costs only $3.95 *including processing!*

Ease? With the Brownie Movie Camera, home movies are simple as snapshots. But get the whole story for yourself from your Kodak dealer.

Movies at snapshot cost! Brownie Movie Camera only $39.75.

Loads easily—no threading. Built-in exposure guide...fine, fast *f*/2.7 lens. Unbeatably low priced at $39.75. Same camera with super-speed *f*/1.9 lens, only $49.50. Either model gives you sharp, clear, full-color movies at the touch of a button. See the "Brownies" soon. Many Kodak dealers offer convenient terms.

"Brownie" movies start to finish! Brownie Movie Projector shows all 8mm. movies crisp, bright...stills, reverse action, too! Only $62.50. Brownie Projection Screen...beaded...a full 30 inches wide. $4.50.

20,000 Leagues Under the Sea by
Walt Disney/ Buena Vista.

Creature From the Black Lagoon
by Universal.

Them by Warner Bros.

Target Earth by Monogram Pictures.

Indoor snapshots—as easy to get as the ones outdoors.

Life's happiest moments so often occur indoors. And now they're yours to keep.

With today's flash cameras, you always get the right amount of light where you want it, when you want it. You're just as sure of good pictures indoors as out.

Nothing new to learn. Just press the button on your camera, the flash bulb goes off automatically, and you've got your picture.

So don't pass up those priceless moments. See your Kodak dealer soon.

It's simple—it's sure—it's so inexpensive—the Brownie Hawkeye Camera, Flash Model, only $7.20 including Federal Tax. Flasholder, $4. Just put on the Flasholder, pop in a flash bulb, and shoot.

New, thrifty Duo-Pak holds two rolls of Kodak Verichrome Film for black-and-white snapshots. One for your camera...one for a spare. In the popular sizes 620, 120, and 127.

The Lord of the Rings Trilogy

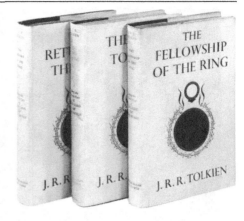

The Lord of the Rings, a series of three fantasy novels written by English author J.R.R. Tolkien, was conceived as a sequel to his 1937 novel *The Hobbit*.

Originally written as one volume, the work was published as a trilogy with *The Fellowship of the Ring* released in July 1954. The second and third books, *The Two Towers* and *The Return of the King*, followed in late 1954 and 1955.

The Lord of the Rings immediate success was credited with the growing popularity of the fantasy genre from the '50s and '60s till the present day. Its influence on popular culture has been wide ranging, spawning many imitators in film, literature and video-gaming.

From 2001-2003 the books were released as a film series directed by Peter Jackson. Shot entirely in New Zealand, the films were a major critical and financial success. Each film garnered several Academy Awards, placing them among the greatest film trilogies ever made.

The Lord of the Rings has been translated in 38 different languages and sold over 150 million copies, remaining popular till this day. The books have been adapted for radio, theater, television and film. In 2003, the trilogy was awarded BBC's Best British novel of all time.

"I had no idea ale was so wonderful."

"It isn't ordinarily; that's Ballantine Ale"

BALLANTINE ALE...the light ale America prefers by 4 to 1!

"I had no idea ale was so wonderful."
"It isn't ordinarily; that's Ballantine Ale"

The popular host these days is likely to be found behind a well-filled tray of sparking *green* bottles...serving his guest Ballantine–the *light* ale.

This delightfully different ale...so light and refreshing...blessed with such an abundance of flavor, of goodness and character...has become America's favorite by four to one.

Next time, do your guests proud. Make it Ballantine Ale all around...the light ale millions prefer. It gives you so much more...in flavor and satisfaction.

Ballantine Ale...the light ale America prefers by 4 to1!

Musical Memories

Music of the early '50s was smooth and mellow, with lyrics focused on story telling and expressing heartfelt emotion. Frank Sinatra, Dean Martin, Bing Crosby, Perry Como, Nat King Cole, Tony Bennett, Sammy Davis Jr. and Charles Azanavour headed the line-up of early '50s classic pop crooners. Their velvety voices led us to joyous highs and the depths of despair. We had yet to fully embrace the electrifying beats of rock 'n' roll.

Music of the early '50s fell into one of three distinct styles– country, R&B, and pop music. In 1954, there was little cross over between the styles. Radio stations focused on one genre, allowing listeners easy access to their preferred type of music.

Bing Crosby, 1951.

Eddie Fisher and actress Debbie Reynolds at their wedding, 1955.

Teen idol Eddy Fisher released ten singles in 1954, in addition to hosting his own variety TV series *Coke Time with Eddie Fisher* (NBC. 1953–1957).

In future years, his good looks and popularity would be over-shadowed by his controversial private life. He is now best remembered for his high-profile marriages to actresses Debbie Reynolds and Elizabeth Taylor.

A Rock 'n' Roll Revolution

Beginning in 1954, rock 'n' roll exploded onto our airwaves and took the world by storm. The energy, the rhythm, the emotion–we'd never heard anything quite like it before. Parents were alarmed and appalled in equal measure. It sprang from the ghettos of small town shop-front record studios while the big city record labels were napping.

Rock 'n' roll was the first music ever created specifically for teenagers. The first of the Baby Boomers had found their sound. It was neither black nor white. It gave expression to youth of any race and social status. It was a mash of rhythm & blues, country & western, gospel, hill-billy, blues, and jazz, with a heavy rock beat.

Chuck Berry, Fats Domino, Bill Haley and His Comets, Jerry Lee Lewis, and of course Elvis, became household names.

Bill Haley and His Comets.

Jerry Lee Lewis.

20th May– *Rock Around the Clock* was released by Bill Haley and His Comets to little fanfare. The single was later adopted as the opening song for the 1955 teen movie *Blackboard Jungle*, sending it straight to number 1 on the music charts. It is widely recognized as marking the birth of rock 'n' roll.

Sun Records in Memphis TN was home to many rock 'n' roll greats, including Elvis Presley, Jerry Lee Lewis, Johnny Cash, Carl Perkins, Roy Orbison, The Dixie Cups, and Howlin' Wolf.

Start your summer fun now with a new RCA Victor portable radio

Extra powerful! RCA Victor "Globe Trotter" picks up stations far beyond the range of ordinary portables. Plays instantly on AC, DC or battery. Has famous "Golden Throat" tone. In smart dove-grey plastic. Model 2BX63, $49.95

It's lighter than you think...and little as a book! The Super "Personal" is only six inches high. Plays instantly, without warm-up. Has new Battery Life Saver Switch. Choice of six colors. Model 2B400 Series, $29.95

Instant performance on AC, DC or battery with the new RCA Victor "Yachtsman." Powerful, built-in Magic Loop antenna and famous "Golden Throat" tone system. Choice of brown or green plastic. Model 3BX51 Series, $34.95

Powered to pick up the world! The RCA Victor "Strato-World"—new 7-band AM/short-wave portable—plays on AC, DC or battery. Genuine cowhide case with scuff-resistant plastic ends. (Alligator-finished cowhide extra.) Model 3BX671, $139.95

You can see how *little* these portables are...how *bright* they look. But just wait till you hear the "size" and "brilliance" of their sound! It's almost unbelievable how the tiny RCA miniature tubes in these new radios have put so much power into so little space. Get set for summer—pick from the "pick of the portables" at your RCA Victor dealer's *now!*

RCA Victor—"the Pick of the Portables"

1954 Billboard Top 30 Songs

	Artist	Song Title
1	Kitty Kallen	Little Things Mean A Lot
2	Perry Como	Wanted
3	Rosemary Clooney	Hey There
4	Crew Cuts	Sh-Boom
5	Jo Stafford	Make Love To Me
6	Eddie Fisher	Oh! My Pa-pa
7	Four Knights	I Get So Lonely
8	Four Aces	Three Coins In The Fountain
9	Doris Day	Secret Love
10	Archie Bleyer	Hernando's Hideaway

Perry Como, 1956.

Eddie Fisher, 1960.

Jo Stafford, 1956.

Doris Day, 1957.

	Artist	Song Title
11	Frank Sinatra	Young At Heart
12	Rosemary Clooney	This Ole House
13	Eddie Fisher	I Need You Now
14	Patti Page	Cross Over The Bridge
15	Gaylords	The Little Shoemaker
16	Dean Martin	That's Amore
17	Frank Weir	The Happy Wanderer
18	Nat King Cole	Answer Me My Love
19	Tony Bennett	Stranger In Paradise
20	Doris Day	If I Give My Heart To You

Tony Bennett.

Nat King Cole, 1958.

	Artist	Song Title
21	Kay Starr	If You Love Me (Really Love Me)
22	Ralph Marterie	Skokiaan
23	Don Cornell	Hold My Hand
24	Patti Page	Changing Partners
25	Perry Como	Papa Loves Mambo
26	Bill Haley and His Comets	Shake, Rattle And Roll
27	Tony Bennett	Rags To Riches
28	Kitty Kallen	In The Chapel In The Moonlight
29	Four Aces	Stranger In Paradise
30	Tony Martin	Here

* From the *Billboard* top 30 singles of 1954.

Fresh and colorful as spring...these four new electrics by Westclox

What more appropriate time to present these wonderful bright new additions to the Westclox family of electric clocks...all abloom with gay Springtime colors and fresh, modern lines. Each has its own personality–all clearly make perfect houseguests whose welcome will never wear out. Meet them soon. You will surely want them to come for a long, long visit where you live.

Manor Electric Wall Clock. Your choice of red, green, yellow or white in this wonderfully adaptable wall clock. Mounts flush. Cleans easily. $3.98. In chrome, a dollar more.

Byron Electric Alarm. Tilt-base makes smart, simple dial easy to read. Gold-colored Roman numerals make handsome contrast with red, green or silver color case. Plain dial. Bell alarm $10.95.

Country Club Electric Alarm. Simple, clean lines show off handsome ivory or green case. Cheerful bell alarm. $9.45. With luminous dial, one dollar more.

Kendall Electric Alarm. Beautifully fashioned wood case in mahogany or blond finish, suits any decor. Pleasant-tone bell alarm. $7.95. Luminous dial, a dollar more.

JUNIOR WHIRLERS!

Your Junior budget never bought more fashion in cottons! Prettiest young patterns and full dancing skirts. Amazing '54 buys!

ONLY **3.98** EACH

DESCRIBED ON PAGE 44

Fashions from *Aldens* home shopping catalog, Summer 1954.

Fashion Trends of the 1950s

With the misery and bleakness of the war years behind us, it was now time to show off. Consumerism was a way of life and we were all too willing to spend money on luxuries, non-essentials, and fashion.

How we looked and how we dressed became important everyday considerations for women and men. We spent money like never before, guided by our favorite fashion icons, and helped along by a maturing advertising industry which flooded us with fashion advice through newspapers, magazines, billboards, radio and television.

Dress by Anne Fogarty, Summer 1954.

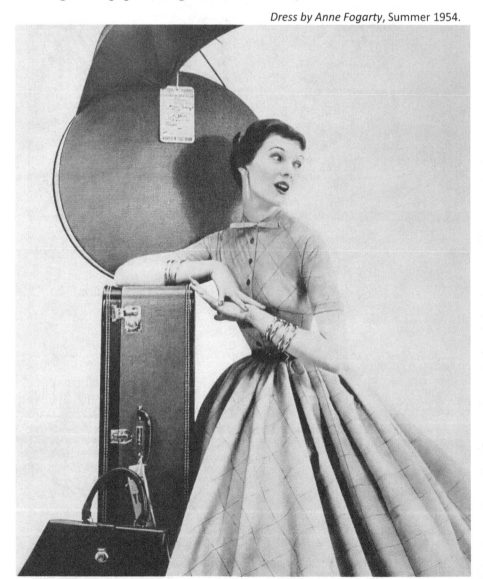

Clothing manufacturers had perfected mass production techniques while providing military uniforms during the war years. They now shifted their focus to well made, stylish, ready-to-wear clothes.

Charm magazine cover, October 1954.

Vogue magazine cover, 1st October 1954.

Seventeen magazine cover, March 1954.

Fashion was no longer a luxury reserved for the wealthy. Now the growing middle class could also afford to be fashionable. Magazines and mail-order catalogs kept us informed of the latest trends in fashion, make-up, and accessories.

Empire Line
20-Gore Skirt
$6.98
[A]

A NEW DRAMA

starring taffeta and lace...
more glamorous than ever

Lace-Frosted
Gown; Stole
$14.98
2 Pcs.
[B]

RHINESTONE-
SPARKED

Also
Half
Sizes

DESCRIBED ON PAGE 18

Sequin-
Embroidered
$9.98
[C]

Part NYLON
Lace
$8.98
[D]

MISSES'
SIZES

Also
Half
Sizes

19

Dresses from the *Bellas Hess* mail order catalog in the "New Look"
style that was popular in the year 1954.

A quick click adjusts each cup
to fit your contours, to give you
exactly-right-for-you uplift!

Bra-O-matic Longline, too...
smooths you, shapes you for the
new figure-hugging silhouettes.

The most exciting advance in bras! Gives
better than custom-fit because *you* adjust
each cup...anytime. Adjusts to any dress
neckline, too.

And it's a beauty! Bandeau in nylon lace or
taffeta with nylon marquisette...plus
stay-in-place nylon leno elastic back
and band. Longline in nylon lace with
acetate satin panels; nylon leno
elastic back and inserts. All with
circle-stitched 4-section cups to
hold their shape...and yours!

BANDEAU $5.95
A, B and C cups; sizes 32 to 40

LONGLINE $8.95
B and C cups; sizes 34 to 42

*bra-O-matic by *Exquisite Form*

A quick click adjusts each cup to fit your contours, to give you
exactly-right-for-you uplift!

Bra-O-matic Longline, too...smooths you, shapes you for the new figure-hugging silhouettes.

The most exciting advance in bras! Gives *better* than custom-fit because *you* adjust each cup...anytime. Adjusts to any dress neckline, too.

And it's a beauty! Bandeau in nylon lace or taffeta with nylon marquisette...plus stay-in-place nylon leno elastic back and band. Longline in nylon lace with acetate satin panels; nylon leno elastic back and inserts. All with circle-stitched 4-section cups to hold their shape...and yours!

Bandeau $5.95. A, B and C cups; sizes 32 to 40.

Longline $8.95. B and C cups; sizes 34 to 42.

Christian Dior's "New Look" from 1947.

The New Look in *Vanity Fair*, May 1953.

As with before the war, all eyes looked to Paris for new trends in haute couture. In 1947 Christian Dior didn't disappoint, unveiling his ultra-feminine, glamorous, extravagant, "New Look".

Gone were the boxy tailored jackets with padded shoulders and slim, short skirts. Paris had brought back femininity, with clinched waists, fuller busts and hips, and longer, wider skirts.

By 1954, dresses reached voluminous proportions with pleats and folds flaunting an abundance of fabric. The New Look set the standard for the entire decade of the 1950s.

EVEN THE WIRE IS CURVED TO STAY UP!

CELEBRITY does more than give you deep-plunging separation . . . CELEBRITY curves the wiring of this strapless bra to make the uplift STAY UP! No tugging, no pulling, no displacement! Get marvelous up-curve flattery in heavenly comfort. White rayon satin, or white cotton.

A Cup,
sizes 32 to 36
B Cup,
sizes 32 to 38

$1.50

Celebrity
"CONTOUR-CURVE STITCHING"
from the bottom up

To achieve this impossible hourglass figure, corsets and girdles were sold in record numbers. Metal underwire bras made a comeback, and a new form of bra known as the "cathedral bra" or "bullet bra" became popular.

Despite criticisms against the extravagance of the New Look, and arguments that heavy corsets and paddings undermined the freedoms women had won during the war years, the New Look was embraced on both sides of the Atlantic. Before long, inexpensive, ready-to-wear versions of Dior's New Look had found their way into our department store catalogs.

Patterns from *Haslam Dresscutting Book No. 31*, Summer 1954.

SACONY SUITS HAVE SUCH FEMININE DETAILS AS SCALLOPED YOKES, CURVING HIPLINES, TURNED-BACK CUFFS. ALL THESE SUITS MADE IN WORSTED FABRICS. 49.95 EACH.

Sacony brings back the ladylike suit

SOFTENED WORSTEDS AT 49.95 EXEMPLIFY NEW TREND

After a season or two of casual under-dressing, women are flocking into suit departments again. And the suits they are choosing have a quieted-down elegance that can best be described as ladylike. However, there is one drawback to this newly gentle mood of dressing. It relies more on meticulous tailoring than flamboyant style, therefore tends to command fancy prices. The notable exception is the new collection Sacony has turned out to sell at 49.95. These suits, some of which are shown above, come in well-chosen worsted fabrics, so competently tailored that the suits retain their soft feminine outline even when suspended from hangers. And Sacony expects to see them worn with flirtatious little hats and spindly-heeled shoes. To assure proper fit, several styles come in petite as well as misses sizes, others in women's half-sizes. All are available in stores around the country, or write Sacony, College Point, Long Island, New York.

Sacony suits have such feminine details as scalloped yokes, curving hiplines, turned-back cuffs. All these suits made in worsted fabrics. 49.95 each.

Sacony brings back the ladylike suit

Softened worsteds at 49.95 exemplify new trend

After a season or two of casual under-dressing, women are flocking into suit departments again. And the suits they are choosing have a quieted-down elegance that can best be described as ladylike. However, there is one drawback to this newly gentle mood of dressing. It relies more on meticulous tailoring than flamboyant style, therefore tends to command fancy prices. The notable exception is the new collection Sacony has turned out to sell at 49.95. These suits, some of which are shown above, come in well-chosen worsted fabrics, so competently tailored that the suits retain their soft feminine outline even when suspended from hangers. And Sacony expects to see them worn with flirtatious little hats and spindly-heeled shoes. To assure proper fit, several styles come in petite as well as misses sizes, others in women's half-sizes. All are available in stores around the country, or write Sacony, College Point, Long Island, New York.

Dior also created a slimmed down alternative look, widely copied by other designers in ready-to-wear outfits and pattern books. This figure-hugging, groomed and tailored look continued to place emphasis on the hourglass figure, and was suitable for day or evening dress, or as an elegant straight skirt and short jacket.

Known as the "sheath dress" or "wiggle dress", this sexier figure-hugging silhouette was preferred by movie stars such as Marilyn Monroe.

Women embraced the femininity of 1950s fashion from head to toe. Hats, scarves, belts, gloves, shoes, stockings, handbags and jewelry were all given due consideration.

Out on the street, no outfit would be complete without a full complement of matching accessories.

Not much changed in the world of men's fashion during the 1950s. Business attire shifted just a little. Suits were slimmer, and ties were narrower. Skinny belts were worn over pleated pants. Hats, though still worn, were on the way out.

Marlon Brando.

Frank Sinatra.

James Dean.

For the younger generation however, the fashion icons of the day set the trends. James Dean and Marlon Brando made the white T-shirt and blue jeans the must-have items in casual attire. Worn alone, or under an unbuttoned shirt or jacket, the look made working class style a middle-class fashion statement.

Exciting new way to see the Northwest

Vista-Domes have just been added to the faster North Coast Limited!

You see rugged snow-capped peaks soaring high above you—white water tumbling through evergreen forests far below. Stretching out before you, and all around you, there's a broad, breathtaking panorama of plains and mountains, forests and rivers.

From the North Coast Limited's new Vista-Domes you see the Northwest as you never could see it before!

You travel in easy-chair comfort, too—in restful, reclining Day-Nite Coach seats or in private-room Pullmans. You enjoy old-

fashioned western hospitality in handsome new surroundings—Dome cars, lounge and dining cars designed by Raymond Loewy.

You speed smoothly along without a worry. Between Chicago and the North Pacific Coast you can really relax—every mile of the way!

Want a preview of the exciting trip you can take on the Vista-Dome North Coast Limited? Write today for your free copy of "Northwest Adventure." Address G. W. Rodine, Passenger Traffic Manager, Room 920 . . .

NORTHERN PACIFIC RAILWAY, St. Paul 1, Minn.

MAIN STREET OF THE NORTHWEST

Exciting new way to see the Northwest

Vista-Domes have just been added to the faster North Coast Limited! You see rugged snow-capped peaks soaring high above you—white water tumbling through evergreen forests far below. Stretching out before you, and all around you, there's a broad, breathtaking panorama of plains and mountains, forests and rivers.

From the North Coast Limited's new Vista-Domes you see the Northwest as you never could see it before!

You travel in easy-chair comfort, too—in restful, reclining Day-Nite Coach seats or private-room Pullmans. You enjoy old-fashioned western hospitality in handsome new surroundings—Dome cars, lounge and dining cars designed by Raymond Loewy.

You speed smoothly along without a worry. Between Chicago and the North Pacific Coast you can really relax—every mile of the way!

Want a preview of the exciting trip you can take on the Vista-Dome North Coast Limited? Write today for your free copy of "Northwest Adventure." Address G.W. Rodine, Passenger Traffic Manager, Room 920...

For the woman looking for beauty as well as comfort

Natural Poise

Beautiful shoes with a made-to-measure fit

All you see is smartness...but the feel is a sweet surprise. Because Natural Poise Shoes, with all their fashion-trim flattery, give you a unique combination of comfort extras. Made over the Dimensional Equalizer Last, they fit as if they were patterned after your own two feet, flex with such freedom...and with cushioned insoles for buoyant walking ease. Choose Natural Poise in Spring's newest colors, in fine, supple leathers...detailed to look much more expensive, they're value-priced to fit any budget.

Technology and Medicine

21st Jan– First Lady Mamie Eisenhower launched USS Nautilus–the world's first nuclear-powered submarine–in Groton, Connecticut. The submarine was commissioned to the US Navy in September, and stayed in operation until 1980.

27th Jun– The world's first nuclear power station opened in Obninsk, Russia.

29th Sep– The European Organization for Nuclear Research (CERN) was founded by twelve European states. The organization has since grown to 23 member nations with its headquarters near Geneva, Switzerland. It remains focused on high-energy particle physics research.

16th Dec– The first synthetic diamond was produced in a laboratory by Tracy Hall for General Electric. Synthetic diamonds would only be used for industrial purposes until the 1970s, when a superior gem-quality form could be manufactured.

23rd Dec– The world's first successful kidney transplant was performed in Boston, Massachusetts, by Dr. Joseph Murray and J. Hartwell Harrison. The medical team avoided organ rejection by using an identical twin as the donor for the recipient.

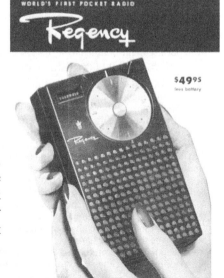

WORLD'S FIRST POCKET RADIO

Regency

$49⁹⁵
less battery

November– The Regency TR-1, made by Texas Instruments, became the first commercially manufactured transistor radio. A total of only 150,000 units were sold, due in part to it being very expensive at $49.95, and to poor sound quality.

MRS. DORIAN MEHLE OF MORRISVILLE, PA., IS ALL THREE: A HOUSEWIFE, A MOTHER, AND A VERY LOVELY LADY.

"I wash 22,000 dishes a year... but I'm proud of my pretty hands !"

You and Dorian Mehle have something in common. Every year, you wash a stack of dishes a quarter-mile high!

Detergents make your job so much easier. They cut right into grease and grime. They get you through dishwashing in much less time. But here's the sad part. While detergents are dissolving grease, they're also taking away the natural oils and youthful softness of your hands!

Yet Dorian hasn't given up detergents. And if she could step off the printed page, you'd find that her hands are as soft, as smooth, as young-looking as a teenager's. Her secret is no secret at all. It's the world's best known beauty routine. It's pure white Jergens Lotion, after every chore.

When you smooth on Jergens Lotion, this liquid formula doesn't just "coat" your hands. It penetrates right away, to help replace that softening moisture your skin needs.

Jergens Lotion has two ingredients doctors recommend for softening. Women must be recommending it, too, for more women use it than any other hand care in the world.

Dorian's husband is the best testimonial to Jergens Lotion care. After years of married life, he still loves to hold her hands!

So keep detergents on the job in your house. Just keep Jergens Lotion there, too. Use it like a prescription: three times a day, after every meal!

Use JERGENS LOTION – avoid detergent hands

Mrs. Dorian Mehle of Morrisville, PA., is all three: a housewife, a mother, and a very lovely lady.

"I wash 22,000 dishes a year...but I'm proud of my pretty hands!"

You and Dorian Mehle have something in common. Every year, you wash a stack of dishes a quarter-mile high!

Detergents make your job so much easier. They cut right into grease and grime. They get you through dishwashing in much less time. But here's the real sad part. While detergents are dissolving grease, they're also taking away the natural oils and youthful softness of your hands!

Yet Dorian hasn't given up detergents. And if she could step off the printed page, you'd find that her hands are as soft, as smooth, as young-looking as a teenager's. Her secret is no secret at all. It's the world's best known beauty routine. It's pure white Jergens Lotion, after every chore.

When you smooth on Jergens Lotion, this liquid formula doesn't just "coat" your hands. It penetrates right away, to help *replace* that softening moisture your skin needs.

Jergens Lotion has two ingredients doctors recommend for softening. Women must be recommending it, too, for more women use it than any other hand care in the world.

Dorian's husband is the best testimonial to Jergens Lotion care. After years of married life, he still loves to hold her hands!

So keep detergents on the job in your house. Just keep Jergens Lotion there, too. Use it like a prescription: three times a day, after every meal!

Sporting Events from 1954

6th May– British athlete Roger Bannister became the first runner to record a mile in under 4 minutes. He clocked 3:59.4 at Iffley Road Track, Oxford, UK. Seven weeks later in Finland, Australian John Landy became the second man to break the 4-minute mile, when he clocked 3:57.9. The two runners would race against each other in August at the British Commonwealth Games, with Bannister taking home the gold.

29th May– British athlete Diane Leather became the first woman to record a mile in under 5 minutes (4:59.6).

13th May–Robin Roberts, baseballer for the Philadelphia Phillies, retired 27 Cincinnati Reds batsmen in a row, a career highlight.

3rd Jul–American tennis prodigy Maureen Connolly won her 3rd consecutive Wimbledon Women's Singles title, beating fellow American Louise Brough 6-2, 7-5. Two weeks later, aged 19, her tennis career would come to a halt following a horse-riding accident which left her with compound fractures to her leg. Connolly had won nine Gram Slam Singles tournaments, including 50 consecutive singles matches in her short-lived career.

30th Jul-7th Aug– 662 athletes from 24 nations took part in the 1954 British Empire and Commonwealth Games held in Vancouver, Canada.

7th Aug– British athlete Jim Peters failed to finish the men's marathon at the 1954 British Empire and Commonwealth Games. Peters entered the stadium 17 minutes ahead of any rival, but collapsed multiple times in an effort to reach the finish line. He was taken to hospital, severely dehydrated and arrived unconscious. Peters had set four world marathon records during his brilliant running career.

Other News from 1954

10th Jan– A BOAC de Havilland Comet plane, traveling from Singapore to London, disintegrated in mid-air and crashed into the Mediterranean Sea. The passenger plane, flight BA781, had made seven transit stops, and was on its last leg from Rome to London. All 35 people on board were killed. The plane had suffered explosive decompression due to structural failures. It was the third Comet built, and the second in a series of three fatal accidents within the span of 12 months.

8th Apr– Another de Havilland Comet plane disintegrated and crashed into the Mediterranean Sea. Structural failures were again blamed. The BOAC charter plane, flight SA201, was flying from Rome to Cairo. Flights BA781 and SA201 had been examined by the same crew of BOAC engineers before departing from Rome airport.

11th Jan– Two avalanches slammed the village of Blons in Austria. The first struck at 9.36am and the second at 7pm. Many of the rescue workers digging out survivors from the first avalanche were buried by the second. In and around Blons, a total of 270 people were buried, of whom 125 died. The avalanches also killed 500 cattle, and destroyed 55 houses and hundreds of farm buildings.

25th Feb– Colonel Gamal Abdal Nasser proclaimed himself Prime Minister of Egypt. Following a failed assassination attempt against him in October, Nassar removed President Mahamed Naguib from power, dismissed Naguib's loyal officers, arrested thousands of dissenters, and assumed leadership of the country. Elections held in 1956 would formalize Nassar's position as President of Egypt. He remained President until his death in 1970.

24th Aug– Getúlio Vargas, Brazilian president from 1930-1945 and again from 1951-1954, was found dead in his bedroom at the presidential palace by a gunshot wound to the chest. His suicide note was found and read to the public by radio broadcast. Vargas had been under pressure from the military to leave power, and had been blamed for conspiring in an assassination attempt on his political rival Carlos Lacerda.

24th Aug– US President Eisenhower signed the *Communist Control Act*, outlawing the Communist Party. Membership of any organization that supported the communist cause became a criminal offense. In September, Eisenhower strengthened the *Espionage & Sabotage Act* to permit the death penalty or life imprisonment in peacetime as well as during wartime, for the crimes of espionage or sabotage. Both acts were passed at the height of McCarthy's Red Scare.

31st Aug-11th Sept– Two Category 3 hurricanes battered the US East Coast causing widespread flooding and power outages, and destroying properties, farm lands and trees. On 31st August, Hurricane Carol made landfall in New England, flooding Connecticut, Long Island, and Rhode Island, and causing widespread damage in Maine and south east Canada. 4,000 homes were destroyed, plus nearly as many boats and cars. 60 deaths were recorded. On 11th September, Hurricane Edna struck Massachusetts, flooding Martha's Vineyard, Nantucket, Cape Cod, Long Island and Rhode Island. A further 20 deaths were recorded.

26th Sep– Gale force winds from Typhoon Marie dragged the Japanese ferry Tōya Maru onto rocks, causing it to capsize and sink near Hokkaido in Japan's north. More than 1,100 people drowned.

25th Oct–Violent storms causing flooding and landslides hit the province of Salerno in southern Italy, killing 263 people.

5th Oct– Hurricane Hazel, at Category 4, was the deadliest hurricane of the season. Fatalities included 1,000 in Haiti, 95 in the USA (from South Carolina upward to the Canadian border), and 85 in Canada. In Haiti, Hazel destroyed 40% of the coffee trees and 50% of the cacao crop, affecting the Haitian economy for several years.

A Dixie Cup Dispenser in your kitchen saves all this work...

- No more between-meal dishwashing!
- No more glasses to be dried and put-away!
- No more broken glasses!
- No more piled-up sinks after late-hour snacks, or after-school milk!
- Dixie Dispenser mounts on any wall or cabinet in a jiffy!

Look for the big economy size...the thrifty way to buy Dixie Cups for everyday home use.

Now at a price you can afford for everyday home use!

Famous People Born in 1954

12th Jan– Howard Stern, American radio DJ.

17th Jan– Robert F. Kennedy Jr., American lawyer, political candidate & writer.

26th Jan– Kim Hughes, Australian cricket batsman & captain.

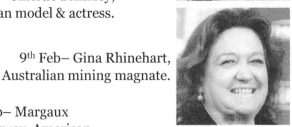

29th Jan– Oprah Winfrey, American TV talk show host.

2nd Feb– Christie Brinkley, American model & actress.

9th Feb– Gina Rhinehart, Australian mining magnate.

16th Feb– Margaux Hemingway, American actress (d.1966).

23rd Feb– Viktor Yushchenko, Ukrainian politician & President (2005-10).

18th Feb– John Travolta, American actor & singer.

23rd Apr– Michael Moore, American filmmaker.

7th Apr– Jackie Chan, Hong Kong martial arts actor.

30th Apr– Jane Campion,
New Zealand film director.

29th Feb– Jerry Seinfeld,
American comedian & actor.

17th Jul– Angela Merkel,
German politician, Chancellor
of Germany (2005-2021).

15th Jun– James Belushi,
American actor & comedian.

12th Aug– François Hollande,
President of France (2012-17).

28th Jul– Hugo Chávez,
President of Venezuela
(1998-2013), (d.2013).

16th Aug– James Cameron,
Canadian film director & writer.

15th Aug– Stieg Larsson,
Swedish author.

18th Sep– Tommy
Tuberville, American
football coach & politician.

25th Aug– Elvis Costello,
English singer & songwriter.

10th Oct– David Lee
Roth, American rock
singer (Van Halen).

21st Sep– Shinzō Abe, Prime Minister of Japan (2006-07 & 2012-2020), (d. 2022).

3rd Nov– Adam Ant (Stuart Goddard), British punk rocker.

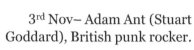
23rd Oct– Ang Lee, Taiwanese American filmmaker.

14th Nov– Bernard Hinault, French cyclist & 5-time Tour de France winner.

8th Nov– Kazuo Ishiguro, British author.

11th Dec– Jermaine Jackson, American singer (Jackson 5).

14th Nov– Condoleezza Rice, 1st female African-American US Secretary of State (2005-09).

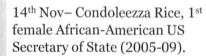

25th Dec– Annie Lennox, Scottish singer (Eurythmics).

21st Dec– Chris Evert, American tennis player.

28th Dec– Denzel Washington, American actor.

26th Dec– Ozzie Smith, American Baseball Hall of Fame infielder.

"Lets play house," said Sue to Tommy, "Dress ol' Spot like Uncle Lou!
"You be Dad, and I'll be Mommy–"And 'Fresh up' just the way <u>they</u> do!"

The All-Family Drink! "Fresh Up" with Seven-Up!

Enjoy sparkling, crystal-clear 7-Up! Seven-Up is so pure, so good, so wholesome that everybody–from the tiniest tots to grandmas and all ages in between–may "fresh up" to his heart's content. And 7-Up makes *food* taste *extra* good. So have a Stackwich with chilled 7-Up. Buy 7-Up where you see the bright 7-Up signs.

You like it...it likes you!

Census Statistics [1]:

- Population of the world   2.72 billion
- Population in the United States   168.74 million
- Population in the United Kingdom   50.89 million
- Population in Canada   15.25 million
- Population in Australia   8.97 million
- Average age for marriage of women   20.3 years old
- Average age for marriage of men   23.0 years old
- Average family income USA $4,200 per year
- Unemployment rate USA   5.0 %

Costs of Goods [2]:

- Average new house $18,281
- Average new car $1,700
- Packard, Clipper $2,638
- A gallon of gasoline $0.29
- Butter $0.59 per pound
- A loaf of bread $0.15
- Bacon $0.87 per pound
- Beef, sirloin steak $0.61 per pound
- Eggs $0.53 per dozen
- Oranges, Florida $0.39 per 5 pounds
- Potatoes $0.29 per 5 pounds
- Soda $0.10 per 12 oz can
- Soap, Ivory $0.25 per 3 cakes
- Movie ticket $1.00

[1] Figures taken from worldometers.info/world-population, US National Center for Health Statistics, *Divorce and Divorce Rates* US (cdc.gov/nchs/data/series/sr_21/sr21_029.pdf) and United States Census Bureau, *Historical Marital Status Tables* (census.gov/data/tables/time-series/demo/families/marital.html).
[2] Figures from thepeoplehistory.com, mclib.info/reference/local-history & dqydj.com/historical-home-prices/.

If you like beer you'll love Schlitz

Satisfaction is what you really want in beer!

Day after day the supreme quality of Schlitz gives more satisfaction to more people than any other beer in the world. It's America's most distinguished beer.

Just the <u>kiss</u> of the hops...No bitterness.

The Beer that Made Milwaukee Famous

This is it! L&M filters are just what the doctor ordered

I smoked filter tip cigarettes for years before I tried L&M's. They have a far better flavor than any other brand of filters I have ever smoked. Read the facts below and try L&M's yourself. You'll like them too. Barbara Stanwyck

This you get...

1. Effective Filtration, from the Miracle Product–Alpha Cellulose–the purest material for filtering cigarette smoke and exclusive to L&M Filters.
2. Selective Filtration–the L&M Filter selects and removes the heavy particles, leaving you a light and mild smoke.
3. Much Less Nicotine–the L&M Filter removes one-third of the smoke, leaves you all the satisfaction.
4. Much More Flavor and Aroma–the right length–the right filter–the right blend of premium quality tobaccos to give you *plenty* of good taste.

Light and Mild. Much More <u>Flavor</u> Much Less <u>Nicotine</u>

These words first appeared in print in the year 1954.

New York minute

CASH FLOW

human growth hormone

HARD COPY

couponing

sleaze

TV dinner

Data Processing

double helix

Black Power

Intensive care

rock and roll

franchisee

Sci-fi

Off-road

HOTLIINE

in vitro fertilization

* From merriam-webster.com/time-traveler/1954.

A heartfelt plea from the author:

I sincerely hope you enjoyed reading this book and that it brought back many fond memories from the past.

Success as an author has become increasingly difficult with the proliferation of **AI generated** copycat books by unscrupulous sellers. They are clever enough to escape copyright action and use dark web tactics to secure paid-for **fake reviews**, something I would never do.

Hence I would like to ask you—I plead with you—the reader, to leave a star rating or review on Amazon. This helps make my book discoverable for new readers, and helps me to compete fairly against the devious copycats.

If this book was a gift to you, you can leave stars or a review on your own Amazon account, or you can ask the gift-giver or a family member to do this on your behalf.

I have enjoyed researching and writing this book for you and would greatly appreciate your feedback.

Best regards,
Bernard Bradforsand-Tyler.

Please leave a
book review/rating at:

https://bit.ly/1954reviews

Or scan the QR code:

Flashback books make the perfect gift-

https://bit.ly/FlashbackSeries

Image Attributions

Photographs and images used in this book are reproduced courtesy of the following:

Page 6 – From *Life* Magazine 20th Sep 1954.
Source: books.google.com/books?id=_IMEAAAAMBAJ&printsec (PD image).*
Page 8 – Nucoa margarine print advertisement From *Life* Magazine 7th Jun 1954. Source: books.google.com/books?id=G1MEAAAAMBAJ&printsec (PD image).*
Page 9 – From *Life* Magazine 8th Jun 1954, source: books.google.com/books?id=3EcEAAAAMBAJ& printsec & 6th Sep 1954, source: books.google.com/books?id=I1QEAAAAMBAJ&printsec (PD images).*
Page 10 – From *Life* Magazine 16th Aug 1954.
Source: books.google.com/books?id=9IMEAAAAMBAJ&printsec (PD image).*
Page 11 – Protest march in St. Louis, MO, 1954. Courtesy of National Archives and Records Administration (PD image). – Magazine cover by Science Service Inc. Source: comicbookplus.com/ ?cbplus=atomic. Pre 1978, no mark (PD image).
Page 12 – From *Life* Magazine 3rd May 1954.
Source: books.google.com/books?id=JIMEAAAAMBAJ&printsec (PD image).*
Page 13 – From *Life* Magazine 8th Mar 1954.
Source: books.google.com/books?id=T0gEAAAAMBAJ&printsec (PD image).*
Page 14 – Leadenhall Street from Bishopsgate, 1955. Creative Commons license. Photo by Ben Brooksbank (PD image).
Page 15 – London aerial by Sunshine34, commons.wikimedia.org/wiki/File:London_1953.jpg. License CC BY-SA 3.0 (PD image). – Classroom, creator unknown. Pre 1978, no copyright mark (PD image).
Page 16 – From *Life* Magazine 17th May 1954.
Source: books.google.com/books?id=IVMEAAAAMBAJ&printsec(PD image).*
Page 17 – Churchill painting, source: en.wikipedia.org/wiki/Winston_Churchill#/media/File:Sir_ Winston_Churchill_-_19086236948.jpg by Yousuf Karsh for Library and Archives Canada, e010751643 (PD image). – Churchill with Queen Elizabeth II, Prince Charles and Princess Anne, 10th Feb 1953. Source: commons.wikimedia.org/wiki/File:Churchill_queen_ Elizabeth_1953.jpg. Pre 1978, no copyright mark (PD image).
Page 18 – From *Life* Magazine 17th May 1954.
Source: books.google.com/books?id=IVMEAAAAMBAJ&printsec (PD image).*
Page 19 – Traffic, creator unknown. Source: theoldmotor.com/?p=171594. Pre 1978 (PD image).
Page 20 – 1954 Mercury Monterey Convertible from *Life* Mag 5th Jul 1954. Source: books.google.com/ books?id=ClQEAAAAMBAJ&printsec (PD image).* – 1954 Dodge Royal from *Life* Mag 17th May 1954. Source: books.google.com/books?id=IVMEAAAAMBAJ&printsec (PD image).* – 1954 Buick Special from *Life* Mag 4th Jan 1954. Source: books.google.com/books?id=i0gEAAAAMBAJ&printsec (PD image).*
Page 21 – Renault 4CV and MG Magnette print magazine advertisements, 1954 (PD image).*
Page 22 – From *Life* Magazine 4th Oct 1954.
Source: books.google.com/books?id=X1IEAAAAMBAJ&printsec (PD image).*
Page 23 – From *Life* Magazine 7th Jun 1954.
Source: books.google.com/books?id=G1MEAAAAMBAJ&printsec (PD image).*
Page 24 – From Life Magazine 2nd Nov 1953.
Source: books.google.com/books?id=IEgEAAAAMBAJ&printsec (PD image).*
Page 25 – Screen still from I Love Lucy, by CBS Broadcasting,** taken from the book I Love Lucy: Celebrating 50 years of Love and Laughter, by Elisabeth Edwards, Running Press Book Publishers, 2010. Source: Library of Congress (097.01.00). [Digital ID # lucy0097_02]. – Screen still from Dragnet, NBC Television** 30th August 1957, source: en.wikipedia.org/wiki/ Dragnet_(1951_TV_series).
Page 26 – Screen still of Steve Allen from Tonight by NBC, 1954.** – Publicity photo for Lassie by CBS, 1954.(PD image).** – Screen still of Attenborough in Zoo Quest by BBC, 1954.** – Father Knows Best publicity photo by CBS, 1954.**
Page 27 – From *Life* Magazine 6th Dec 1954.
Source: books.google.com/books?id=VVIEAAAAMBAJ&printsec (PD image).*
Page 28 – Ivy Mike by The Official CTBTO, 1st Nov 1952. Source: flickr.com/photos/ctbto/6476282811/. – Castle Bravo, creator unknown 1st Mar 1954. Source: commons.wikimedia.org/wiki/Category:Castle_ Bravo. These images are the work of an officer or employee of the US Government as part of that person's official duties, and as such is in the public domain.
Page 29 – Duck and take cover, 1962, by Walter Albertin for NYWT&S newspaper. Source: US Library of Congress, Reproduction number: LC-DIG-ds-01489 (PD image).
Page 30 – Publicity photo for Leonard Bernstein, source: commons.wikimedia.org/wiki/Category: Leonard_Bernstein. – Studio publicity photo for Lena Horne, by MGM. 1946. Source: commons. wikimedia.org/wiki/Category:Lena_Horne. – Orson Welles arriving at Schiphol Airport, by Ben van Meerendonk / AHF, 3rd Feb 1948. Source: commons.wikimedia.org/wiki/Category:Orson_Welles. All photos this page are in the public domain.
Page 31 – Senator McCarthy at the Army-McCarthy hearings, 9th Jun 1954. Source: commons. wikimedia.org/wiki/Category:Joseph_McCarthy (PD image).*
Page 32 – From *Life* Magazine 6th Dec 1954.
Source: books.google.com/books?id=VVIEAAAAMBAJ&printsec (PD image).*

Page 33 – Lawyers Hayes, Marshall and Nabrit at the Supreme Court, 17th May 1954. Source: commons.wikimedia.org/wiki/Category:Brown_v._Board_of_Education (PD image). – Briggs Jnr., Brown Smith, Bolling Jnr., and Belton Brown by Al Ravenna for NYWT&S, Hotel Americana, 9th June 1964. Source: US Library of Congress, Reproduction Number: LC-USZ62-126440 (PD image). Page 34 – The Geneva Conference, source: commons.wikimedia.org/wiki/Category:Geneva_ Conference_(1954). This photo is the work of an officer or employee of the US Government as part of that person's official duties, and as such is in the public domain. – Map of partition of Indochina, by SnowFire. Source: en.wikipedia.org/wiki/1954_Geneva_Conference. CC BY-SA 4.0, ShareAlike 4.0 Int. Page 35 – United Air Lines print advertisement, source: eBay.com (PD image).*
Page 36 – Disney with Orange County officials, source: en.wikipedia.org/wiki/Disneyland (PD image). – Disney, 17th July 1955. Source: thisdayindisneyhistory.com/DisneylandGrandOpening.html. Creator unknown, no copyright mark (PD image). – Ronald Reagan, screen still from Dateline: Disneyland on ABC.** Source: yesterland.com/dl1955.html. – Sketch plan for Disneyland by artist Herb Ryman for Disney Enterprises Inc. Image is reproduced here under USA Fair Use laws due to: 1- image is a low resolution copy; 2- image does not devalue the ability of the copyright holder to profit from the original work in any way; 3- Image is too small to be used to make illegal copies for use in another book; 4- The image is relevant to the article created.
Page 37 – Young girl, source: polioplace.org/history/artifacts/reluctant-poster-child. Pre-1978, no mark (PD image). – Iron Lung ward, source: commons.wikimedia.org/wiki/File:Iron_Lung_ward-Rancho_Los_ Amigos_Hospital.gif by fda.gov (PD image). – Children's ward, source: imgur.com/gallery/vdwfM40. Pre-1978, no copyright mark (PD image).
Page 38 – National Accounting Machine print advertisement, source:eBay. (PD image).*
Page 39 – From *Life* Magazine 8th Feb 1954.
Source: books.google.com/books?id=OkgEAAAAMBAJ&printsec (PD image).*
Page 40 – Screen still from On the Waterfront, by Colombia Pictures 1954.**
Page 41 – Rear Window, 1954 film poster by Paramount Pictures.** – A Star is Born , 1954 film poster by Warner Bros. Pictures.** – White Christmas, 1954 film poster by Paramount Pictures.**
Page 42 – From Life Magazine 3rd May 1954.
Source: books.google.com/books?id=JIMEAAAAMBAJ&printsec (PD image).*
Page 43 – 20,000 Leagues Under the Sea, 1954 movie poster by Walt Disney/ Buena Vista.** – Creature From the Black Lagoon, 1954 movie poster by Universal.** – Them, 1954 movie poster by Warner Bros.** – Target Earth, 1954 movie poster by Monogram Pictures.**
Page 44 – From Life Magazine 1st Feb 1954.
Source: books.google.com.sg/books?id=KEgEAAAAMBAJ&printsec (PD image).*
Page 45 – Lord of the Rings books,** source: abebooks.com/rare-books/most-expensive-sales/year-2015.shtml?cm_sp.
– Lord of the Rings movie posters, 2001-2003, by New Line Cinema.**
Page 46 – From *Life* Magazine 5th Jul 1954.
Source: books.google.com/books?id=ClQEAAAAMBAJ&printsec (PD image).*
Page 47 – Bing Crosby studio portrait from 1951, for CBS. (PD image). – Wedding of Fisher to Reynolds, 1955, creator unknown. Source: commons.wikimedia.org/wiki/Category:Eddie_Fisher (PD image).
Page 48 – Lewis, source: en.wikipedia.org/wiki/Jerry_Lee_Lewis. Pre-1978, no copyright mark (PD image). – Haley, source: commons.wikimedia.org/wiki/Category:Bill_Haley_%26_His_Comets. Pre-1978, no copyright mark (PD image). – Sun Records, source: commons.wikimedia.org/wiki/File: Sun_Studio,_Memphis.jpg. Pre-1978, no copyright mark (PD image).
Page 49 – From *Life* Magazine 17th May 1954.
Source: books.google.com/books?id=IVMEAAAAMBAJ&printsec (PD image).*
Page 50 – Perry Como by NBC Television, 1956. Source: commons.wikimedia.org/wiki/File:Perry_ Como_1956.JPG. – Eddie Fisher studio publicity photo, source: commons.wikimedia.org/wiki/ Category:Eddie_Fisher. – Frankie Laine publicity photo, 1954. Source: en.wikipedia.org/wiki/Frankie_ Laine. – Doris Day promotional photo, 1957. Source: en.wikipedia.org/wiki/Doris_Day. – Jo Stafford, by Colombia Records Feb 1956. Source: commons.wikimedia.org/wiki/File:Jo_Stafford_1956.JPG. All images page permission PD-PRE1978 (PD image).
Page 51– Tony Bennet promotional photo for the song *Rags to Riches*, Colombia Records, 1953. – Nat King Cole publicity for GAC-General Artists Corporation. Source: commons.wikimedia.org/wiki/File: Nat_King_Cole_1958.JPG. (PD image).
Page 52 – From *Life* Magazine 16th Aug 1954.
Source: books.google.com/books?id=9IMEAAAAMBAJ&printsec (PD image).*
Page 53 – Fashions from the *Aldens* mail order catalog, Summer 1954 (PD image).*
Page 54 – From *Vogue* Magazine, Summer 1954. Source: eBay.com (PD image).*
Page 55 – Fashion magazine covers from 1954. Pre 1978, no copyright mark (PD image).*
Page 56 – *Bellas Hess* Catalog, Fall-Winter 1954, (PD image).*
Page 57 – From *Life* Magazine 3rd May 1954.
Source: books.google.com/books?id=JIMEAAAAMBAJ&printsec (PD image).*
Page 58 – From *Vanity Fair,* May 1953. Source: likesoldclothes.tumblr.com/tagged/1953/ (PD image).*

Page 59 – Celebrity advert from *Life* Magazine 1st Jun 1953. Source: books.google.com.sg/books?id=30cEAA AAMBAJ&printsec (PD image).* – *Haslam Dresscutting patterns*, Summer No.31, 1954. Pre 1978 (PD image).*
Page 60 – From Life Magazine 13th Sep 1954.
 Source: books.google.com/books?id=_1MEAAAAMBAJ&printsec (PD image).*
Page 61 – Marilyn Monroe in 1952 studio publicity portrait for film Niagara, by 20th Century Fox. (PD image). – Models walking photo. Source: Jessica at myvintagevogue.com. Licensed under CC BY 2.0.
Page 62 – Sinatra, creator unknown. Source: morrisonhotelgallery.com/collections/wtvp8g/The-Sinatra-Experience. – Brando, creator unknown. Source: dailybreak.co/wp-content/uploads/2019/06/Marlon-Brando-Ford-Thunderbird-1955-Est.-2444.jpg. – Dean, creator unknown. Source: en.wikipedia.org/wiki/James_Dean. All images this page Pre-1978, no copyright mark (PD image).
Page 63 – 1954 Vista-Dome print advertisement (PD image).*
Page 64 – From *Good Housekeeping* Magazine, Mar 1954 (PD image).*
Page 65 – Nautillus, by US Navy photographer, 17th Jan 1955 (PD image). – Printer advertisement for The Regency TR-1 by Texus Instruments (PD image).*
Page 66 – From *Life* Magazine 11th Jan 1954.
Source: books.google.com/books?id=vkgEAAAAMBAJ&printsec (PD image).*
Page 67 – Maureen Connolly, source: commons.wikimedia.org/wiki/Category:Maureen_Connolly (PD image). – Jim Peters at the British Commonwealth Games, Vancouver, 7th Aug 1954. Still image from video of the race.
Page 68 – Blons Avalanche, 11th Jan 1954. Foto: Helmut Klapper, Vorarlberger Landesbibliothek. Source: en.wikipedia.org/wiki/1954_Blons_avalanches (PD image). – Getúlio Vargas, portrait 1951. Source: commons.wikimedia.org/wiki/Category:Getúlio_Vargas (PD image).
Page 69 – President Eisenhower in the Oval Office, 29th Feb 1956. Source: commons.wikimedia.org/wiki/Dwight_D._Eisenhower (PD image). – Damage caused by Hurricane Hazel, Caronlina Beach, 15th Oct 1954. Photo courtesy of the Wilmington Star News.
Page 70 – From *Life* Magazine 5th Apr 1954.
Source: books.google.com/books?id=W1MEAAAAMBAJ&printsec (PD image).*
Page 71 – From *Life* Magazine 11th Jan 1954.
Source: books.google.com/books?id=vkgEAAAAMBAJ&printsec (PD image).*
Page 72-74– All photos are, where possible, CC BY 2.0 or PD images made available by the creator for free use including commercial use. Where commercial use photos are unavailable, photos are included here for information only under US fair use laws due to: 1- images are low resolution copies; 2- images do not devalue the ability of the copyright holders to profit from the original works in any way; 3- Images are too small to be used to make illegal copies for use in another book; 4- The images are relevant to the article created.
Page 75 – From *Life* Magazine 11th Jan 1954.
Source: books.google.com/books?id=vkgEAAAAMBAJ&printsec (PD image).*
Page 78 – From *Life* Magazine 1st Mar 1954.
Source: books.google.com/books?id=S0gEAAAAMBAJ&printsec (PD image).*
Page 79 – From *Life* Magazine 5th Apr1954.
Source: books.google.com/books?id=W1MEAAAAMBAJ&printsec (PD image).*

*Advertisement (or image from an advertisement) is in the public domain because it was published in a collective work (such as a periodical issue) in the US between 1925 and 1977 and without a copyright notice specific to the advertisement.
**Posters for movies or events are either in the public domain (published in the US between 1925 and 1977 and without a copyright notice specific to the artwork) or owned by the production company, creator, or distributor of the movie or event. Posters, where not in the public domain, and screen stills from movies or TV shows, are reproduced here under USA Fair Use laws due to: 1- images are low resolution copies; 2- images do not devalue the ability of the copyright holders to profit from the original works in any way; 3- Images are too small to be used to make illegal copies for use in another book; 4- The images are relevant to the article created.

Made in United States
North Haven, CT
13 June 2024

53596647R00050